# Note to Parents and Teachers

The READING ABOUT: STARTERS series introduces key science vocabulary and concepts to young children while encouraging them to discover and understand the world around them. The series works as a set of graded readers in three levels.

LEVEL 3: READ ALONE follows guidelines set out in the National Curriculum for Year 3 in schools. These books can be read alone or as part of guided or group reading. Each book has three sections:

• Information pages that introduce key concepts. Key words appear in bold for easy recognition on pages where the related science concepts are explained.
• A lively story that recalls this vocabulary and encourages children to use these words when they talk and write.
• A quiz asks children to look back and recall what they have read.

WHAT IS A SHADOW? looks at LIGHT. Below are some answers and activities related to the questions on the information spreads that parents, carers and teachers can use to discuss and develop further ideas and concepts:

p. 4 *Why are some places dark all the time?* Ask children to think about places where light can't get in, e.g. inside a cave, cupboard or box.

p. 6 *How else can you protect yourself from the Sun?* You can wear a hat to protect your head, a T-shirt to cover your skin and put on sun cream to protect bare skin.

p. 11 *Can you guess what objects are by feeling them?* Ask children to think about how different senses help them to find their way in the day and at night.

p. 13 *Why do we have to be careful near candles?* Flames can burn and if you knock them they could start a fire. You could also mention that candles are useful in a power cut.

p. 15 *Will the silhouette change if the boy puts on a hat?* Yes. You could also ask if the silhouette changes if the boy moves nearer to or further away from the light source.

p. 17 *What do you think happens to your shadow when you jump up in the air?* When your feet leave the ground, they no longer touch your shadow.

p. 19 *When do you cast the shortest shadows?* You cast the shortest shadows when the Sun is highest in the sky – at noon. The longest shadows occur at sunrise and sunset.

p. 21 *When can't you use a sundial during the day?* When it is cloudy.

p. 23 *Which are transparent, translucent or opaque?* Encourage children to make a chart sorting items into groups.

## ADVISORY TEAM

**Educational Consultant**
**Andrea Bright** – Science Co-ordinator, Trafalgar Junior School, Twickenham

**Literacy Consultant**
**Jackie Holderness** – former Senior Lecturer in Primary Education, Westminster Institute, Oxford Brookes University

**Series Consultants**
**Anne Fussell** – Early Years Teacher and University Tutor, Westminster Institute, Oxford Brookes University

**David Fussell** – C.Chem., FRSC

# CONTENTS

© Aladdin Books Ltd 2005

**Designed and produced by**
Aladdin Books Ltd
2/3 Fitzroy Mews
London W1T 6DF

**First published in**
Great Britain in 2005 by
Franklin Watts
96 Leonard Street
London EC2A 4XD

A catalogue record for this
book is available from the
British Library.

ISBN 0 7496 6269 7 (H'bk)

ISBN 0 7496 6384 7 (P'bk)

All rights reserved
Printed in Malaysia

**Editor:** Sally Hewitt
**Design:** Flick, Book Design
and Graphics
**Thanks to:**
• The pupils of Trafalgar Junior
School, Twickenham and St.
Paul's C.E. Primary School,
Addlestone, for appearing as
models in this book.
• Andrea Bright, Janice Bibby and
Stephanie Cox for helping to
organise the photoshoots.
• The pupils and teachers of
Trafalgar Junior School,
Twickenham and St. Nicholas
C.E. Infant School, Wallingford,
for testing the sample books.

**Photocredits:**
*l-left, r-right, b-bottom, t-top,*
*c-centre, m-middle*
Cover b, 24 both, 25b, 26 both,
27ml & br, 28tr — Jim Pipe. Cover
tl & tm, 5r, 31t — Flat Earth.
Cover tr, 3, 13b, 15ml, 16tr, 18bl,
19bl, 31bcr — Photodisc. 2tl, 2bl,
4 both, 5r, 5c, 9bl, 11tr, 11ml,
12tr, 13t, 14tr, 20tr, 22b, 23tl,
31mr, 31bl, 31bcl — Corbis. 2ml,
11br, 15br, 16bl, 17 all, 19ml &
mr, 23br, 28b, 29ml, 29b, 30 both
— Marc Arundale/Select Pictures.
6tr, 7b, 14b, 22tr — DAJ. 6bl,
7tr, 21t, 31ml — Flick Smith.
10l — Comstock. 10r — Brand X
Pictures. 12tml — Select Pictures.
12b — Flat Earth. 15tr — Corel.
18tr, 21b — Stockbyte. 20b,
23mr, 25tr, 29tr, 31br — Ingram
Publishing. 27tr — John Foxx
Images.

LIGHT

# What Is a Shadow?

by Jim Pipe

Aladdin/Watts
London • Sydney

# LIGHT AND DARK

These two pictures show the same place. In this picture it is **light**. You can see trees and animals.

**Light**

**Dark**

Here it is almost **dark**. Without **light**, you can't see anything!

*Places are dark when there is no light. When the Sun sets, it gets dark outside. Why are some places dark all the time?*

During the day, the **light** changes outside.
When the Sun is low, the sky is **darker**.
When the Sun is high, the sky is **lighter**.

### Sunrise
The day starts
to get light
when the Sun
appears.
This is called
sunrise.

### Noon
The sky gets
lighter and
lighter until
noon. This is
the middle of
the day.

### Sunset
Later in the
day, the Sun
appears lower.
When the Sun
has set, it is
dark and night.

# THE SUN

The **Sun** lights up our day.
When it is cloudy, colours look dull.
When the **Sun** shines,
colours look bright.

A sunny day can
cheer you up.
But the **Sun** can
also harm you.

NEVER look
straight at the **Sun**.
It can damage
your eyes.

**Sun**

**Hat**

**Sunglasses**

**T-shirt**

Sunglasses protect your
eyes from bright light.
How else can you protect
yourself from the Sun?

Heat from the **Sun**
can burn your skin.
Rubbing **sun** cream on your
skin helps to protect it.

On a hot day, don't
stay too long in the **Sun**.
Play indoors or find
a place in the shade.

**Sun cream**

**In the shade**

# STARS AND MOON

The Sun is a **star** just like the **stars** that twinkle in the night sky.

But the Sun is much closer to Earth than any other **star**. That is why it is so bright.

**Sun shines**

**Sun's light**

Many groups of stars have names. This group of stars is Orion.

Remember this shape and see if you can spot this group of stars in the sky at night.

**Group of stars**

The Earth is always spinning.
It spins all the way round once each day.

The Sun can only shine on one side of the
Earth at a time. On this side it is daytime.
On the other side it is dark and night-time.

**Earth spins**

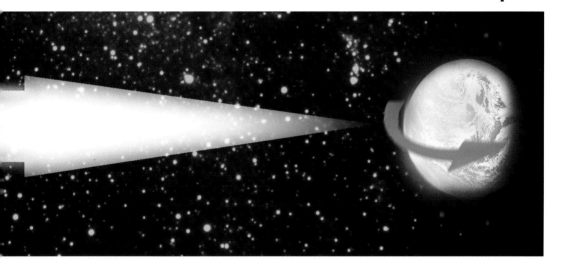

**Moon**

The **Moon** does not
make its own light
like the Sun.

Moonlight is light
from the Sun bouncing
off the **Moon**.

# DAY AND NIGHT

As the Earth spins, it changes from **day** to **night** on your side of the world.

**Day**

**Night**

People cannot see things easily in the dark. So most people work during the **day** when it is light and sleep at **night** when it is dark.

Animals and plants also need the Sun's light to live and grow.

Most animals are busy in the **day**, too. But some animals can see in low light.
They hunt for food at **night**.

The big eyes of this leopard help it to see in the moonlight.

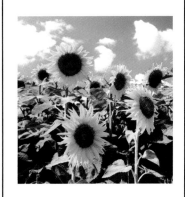

Plants need light from the Sun to grow.

Sunflowers face the Sun to get as much light as they can.

**Leopard**

Put on a blindfold. Ask a friend to put different objects on a table.

Can you guess what objects are by feeling them? Would it be easier to know by seeing them?

# LIGHT SOURCES

During the day our light comes from the Sun. It is a natural **light source**.

When it gets dark at night, we use man-made **light sources**.

Electricity powers the lights in your home and on the streets. This street is lit up by thousands of coloured lights.

A torch is a man-made light source. Its power comes from batteries.

### Street lights

Ask an adult to light a candle for you.
Watch what happens when the flame moves about, or flickers.

Why do we have to be careful near candles?

When things burn they give off light. **Candle**
Before electric lights were invented,
people used candles as **light sources**.

Many people around the world still use fire
as a **light source** as well as for cooking.

**A camp fire**

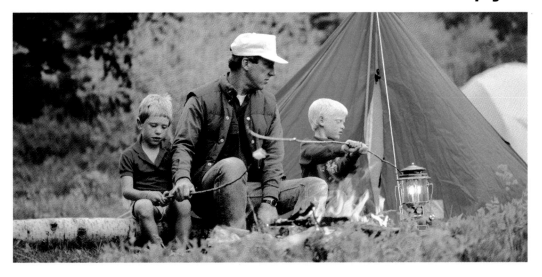

# LIGHT RAYS

Look at light shining through this window.

Can you see that the light travels in straight lines? These lines are called **rays**.

When you stand in the Sun, you block the **light rays** with your body. This makes a dark patch on the ground. This is your shadow.

**Light rays**

**Shadow**

14

Because **light rays** travel in straight lines, they can't bend around objects.

A cave is dark because the **light rays** can't follow it as it twists and turns.

**Cave**

What are these shapes? When we see only the dark side of an object we see its silhouette.

This girl is drawing the silhouette of her friend on a board.

Will the silhouette change if the boy puts on a hat?

**Silhouette**

15

# SHADOWS

Anything that blocks light rays makes a **shadow**. When you move, your shadow does too.

What is making the big **shadow** in this picture?

**Shadow from the Sun**

**Shadow from a light**

This girl is making a big scary **shadow** by standing near to a light.

When she moves away from the light, her **shadow** gets smaller.

16

**Dog**

**Rabbit**

These children are making shapes with **shadows**.
They are using torches and other light sources.

They stand near a wall
to see the **shadow** clearly.

When you stand on the
ground, a shadow always
touches your feet.

What do you think
happens to your shadow
when you jump up
in the air?

This boy is making
his shadow as small
as he can. He is
crouching down on
the ground.

# LONGER AND SHORTER

As the Sun moves across the sky, shadows get **longer** and **shorter**.

But the Sun is not really moving. It's the Earth that moves.

The Sun appears to move because the Earth is spinning around and around.

*Earth spins like a globe*

When the Sun is low in the sky, your body blocks more of the Sun's rays. You cast a **longer** shadow.

In the middle of the day, the Sun appears high in the sky. You block less rays. So you cast a **shorter** shadow.

**Early morning shadow**       **Midday shadow**

At what times of day do you cast the longest shadows?

When do you cast the shortest shadows?

# SUNDIALS

The Sun divides each 24 hours into day and night.

We can guess the time by seeing where the Sun is. We can also use shadows to tell the time.

The upright part of a **sundial** makes a shadow. As the Sun changes position in the sky, this shadow points out the time.

**Sunset**

**Shadow from Sun**

**Sundial**

This boy is making a **sundial**.
First, he puts a tall stick into the ground.

He marks the stick's shadow with a stone.
Every hour he marks the shadow again with
another stone. He writes the hour on each stone.

Tomorrow he can tell the time by seeing
which stone the Sun's shadow points to.

A sundial does not work
at night as there are no
shadows from the Sun.

When can't you use a
sundial during the day?

# TRANSLUCENT AND OPAQUE

A glass window is transparent.
You can see right through it.

**Transparent glass**

Some materials let some light
pass through them. But you
cannot see through them.
They are **translucent**.

**Translucent curtains**

Some objects do not let light through. We say these objects are **opaque**.

**Opaque** objects make shadows when they block light rays. A sun shade blocks most of the Sun's light.

**Opaque sun shade**

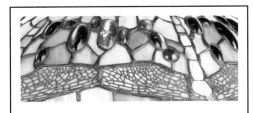

These pieces of coloured glass are translucent.

Look at plastic sweet wrappers, plastic bottles, wood, metal, glass jars and tracing paper. Which are transparent, translucent or opaque?

23

# THE SHADOW PLAY

*Look out for ideas about shadows.*

It was early in the morning and the Sun was low in the sky.

Inside, Chloe was reading the story of Peter Pan. She and her sister Clara were going to put on a shadow play with their cousins Ben and Sharon. Ben had said they should all think of ideas using shadows.

In the story, Peter Pan's shadow is stolen by Wendy's dog, Nana. Luckily, Wendy sews Peter Pan's shadow back on!

"That's a hard story to do," said Chloe.

"I agree," said Clara. "But it's a sunny day. Let's go outside and get some ideas!"

The girls put on their coats.
"The Sun is very bright
today," said Clara.
"I wish I had my sunglasses."

The girls walked outside.
"Look how my shadow always touches my feet,"
said Clara. "Even when I run I can't lose it!"

"Your shadow makes you look taller," said Chloe.
"I'll remember that for our play."

Soon after, Ben and Sharon came over to play.

The Sun was shining through the window.

"I'll show you how to make shadow shapes with your hands," said Ben. "This is a bird."
He moved his hands again. "And this is a dog."

"I can do better than that," said Chloe, picking up her fluffy dog. "You big cheat!" laughed Ben.

Later that day, they watched the Sun going down. "Look at that pretty sunset," said Clara. "I guess that means no more shadows."

"We can use a lamp or a torch instead. Any light will do!" said Sharon.

"You're right. Look!" said Chloe, making a shape with her hand. "This lampshade lets the light through. It's translucent," said Clara.

"I know another trick," said Ben. "Look, our shadows can touch even though we're not."

"Now let's try to make some spooky shapes!" said Sharon.

The next morning, Uncle Justin arrived. He grabbed Clara and gave her a big hug.

"Look, it's a monster with four arms and two heads," shouted Ben.
Uncle Justin and Clara looked around – their two shadows were mixed together!

All the grown-ups went into the kitchen to chat. Ben said, "Let's get on with the play!"

"We made these puppets at school," said Sharon.

Sharon showed them the shapes cut from card. Each shape was taped to a pencil so it was easy to hold.

The children thought about
what story they would do.
"Let's do Jack and the
Beanstalk," said Ben.
"A pot plant can be the beanstalk!"

"Who will be the giant?" asked Clara.

"I've got an idea," said Chloe.

Sharon's dad hung a sheet over
a line. Then he put a bright
light behind the sheet.

The grown-ups sat on a sofa on the other side
of the sheet. Sharon's mum turned out the
main lights. The play was ready to begin.

The four children used a big torch to help them read the story in the dark.

Halfway through the story, Chloe stood up. "Get down. You'll ruin it!" said Ben.

"I'm the *giant*," whispered Chloe. "Next to a puppet, I'm huge!" Everyone agreed that Chloe's shadow made a great giant!

**WRITE YOUR OWN STORY** about shadows. Make a list of the tricks you can play with shadows and see which your friends can do.

| Can you? | Helpful Hints |
|---|---|
| Mix two shadows | Make two shadows shake hands |
| Escape your shadow | Jump in the air |
| Fit inside a friend's shadow | Make yourself as small as you can |
| Make your shadow reach a place you can't go. | Touch the top of a tree's shadow. |
|  |  |

# QUIZ

When does the **Sun** appear low in the sky?

Answer on pages 5 and 19

How does **sun** cream protect your skin?

Answer on page 7

Why does a leopard have big eyes?

Answer on page 11

Can you explain these words?

Rays

Opaque

Silhouette

Sundial

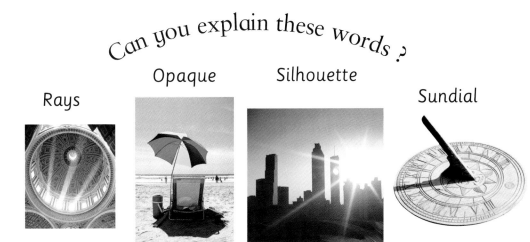

Answers on pages 14, 15, 20, 23

# INDEX